# NORTH EAST SAIL
## *Berwick to King's Lynn*

Sunderland built barque *Sea Breeze*
being towed to Goole

# NORTH EAST SAIL

## Berwick to King's Lynn

Robert Simper

David & Charles

Newton Abbot    London
North Pomfret (VT)  Vancouver

TO JOANNA

ISBN 0 7153 6920 2

Library of Congress Catalog Card Number 74 2046 3

© Robert Simper 1975

Set in 11 on 13pt Baskerville
Photoset and printed in Great Britain
by Redwood Burn Limited
Trowbridge & Esher
for David & Charles (Holdings) Limited
South Devon House Newton Abbot Devon

Published in the United States of America
by David & Charles Inc
North Pomfret Vermont 05053 USA

Published in Canada
by Douglas David & Charles Limited
3645 McKechnie Drive West Vancouver BC

# Contents

# Introduction

In the 1850s the ports of North East England were crammed with sailing ships and sailing fishing craft were drawn up on the beaches of every landing place. Sail was supreme. Looking back we can see that the steamships were steadily improving and were destined to drive sail from the sea, but to the shipowners and seamen of the mid nineteenth century, sail was still practical and was going to continue to be for the next fifty years. But the competition was intense, both from the ever improving steamers and between rival shipowners. Throughout this period sailing ships were constantly being improved to meet new challenges. This struggle between sail and steam very much affected the people and ports of the North East of England. Because many of the shipyards in the region later became renowned for virtually mass producing tramp steamers the story of sail from this coast has been rather overlooked. To try and rectify this the following pages will bring to life something of the merchant and fishing sailing vessels that belonged to the ports and havens between the River Tweed and The Wash from the mid nineteenth century until they finally faded away.

When sailors talked of their days in sail they spoke of it in the same way as old soldiers did when they relived their battles. It had often been hell at the time, but had heightened their lives and set them apart from the humdrum existence of life ashore. Sometimes the harsh reality was a little more than they could take. Certainly the crew of the 395 ton Sunderland barque *Bussorah* felt so when she sailed for China in 1870. The little wooden barque was barely out into the North Sea when seven of the eleven men on board refused to carry out orders. The master had little option but to run into the Humber and anchor off Grimsby. Here the men appeared in court charged with mutiny. The magistrate gave them the opportunity to go back to sea or go to jail. All refused to go back to the ship and they were each given ten weeks on the treadmill. At least they would not drown there, for these were the years when a bad gale in the North Sea could and often did overwhelm a hundred colliers and smacks in a single night. Britain had by far the largest merchant navy in the world but every year about eight per cent of this vast fleet were lost. The fact that the sea took a steady toll of life was accepted, not just by the men, but by their wives and families. Many European seamen liked to remain uncommitted but the seamen of North East England tended to take a wife, which meant that every ship lost deprived several households of its breadwinner. It was an all embracing term this word lost; often when a ship failed to arrive at a port no one knew for certain what had become of her. In some periods an average of six British registered ships were being reported missing every day. Between 1865 and 80 some 32,000 were lost at sea—permanently.

*Lloyds List* reported on average at least one collision at sea every day. Take just one day at one port, Grimsby, 31 August 1873. The timber ship *Wilhelm*

Cobles running pleasure trips at Scarborough

*Tresmeden* came in with damage to her bulwarks and rigging after a collision with an unknown vessel. The same day the *Lucy*, bound in from a Baltic voyage to Riga damaged herself by hitting the pier as she was towed in. Next day the barquentine *Star* limped in with a mast gone after a collision with an unknown vessel near the Inner Dowsing and so it went on every day all along the coast. Often a vessel came in with a report which might be linked with a missing ship like the German brig which on arriving at Newcastle on 2 June 1882 reported seeing an unknown vessel drifting upside down in the North Sea.

Some ships lasted a long time. The South Shields brig *Brotherly Love* was 114 years old when she was run down and sunk off the Yorkshire coast in 1878. With a wooden hull it is possible to go on rebuilding and patching up until none of the original material is left. This goes on as long as the vessel is considered to be of service. This is why the *Brotherly Love* and a few more like her came to last so long. What it really indicates is that the coal trade altered very little throughout this long period. It certainly does not indicate that wood is an indestructible building material. The nineteenth century was full of romantic songs on a

The steel Humber sloop *Ivie*, 1947

theme of 'hearts of oak', a sentiment derived from Nelson's wooden walls at Trafalgar. Winning a decisive battle did not mean that oak could withstand years of the type of rough treatment the coal trade involved. Oak, if it completely looses its sap, tends to go to powder. Some of the pine woods retain their sap and these later came into favour. A wooden hull has about the same life span as a man and that depends on a great many factors, but going back through the records it is surprising how many wooden ships lasted about sixty or seventy years.

It was not decay that cut short the active life of the average trader, but the merciless North Sea. In 1856 alone 536 colliers were lost when they were struggling to make the passage south deeply loaded with coal and another 140 were lost when returning north in ballast. Preparation for death was a subject which featured very vividly in the minds of men in the nineteenth century. Death was so obviously near that no one could completely forget it. For most people life was an uphill grind so that who could blame them for looking forward to receiving their just reward in the next world. They certainly did not get it in this one. Others took comfort in drinking which promised nothing, but gave a more immediate uplift.

Quite a high percentage of ships were lost at sea simply because they should never have been there. Gradually the position was corrected by the Merchant Shipping Acts, but these reforms came too slowly and did not really get at the root of the problem. The Tynemouth shipowner James Hall campaigned against unseaworthy ships and incompetent officers. However when the coal merchant and Member of Parliament for Derby, Samuel Plimsoll, took up the cause, reforms became real. Plimsoll's book *Our Seamen* published in 1873 brought the affair to the public notice. There was a great outcry against the unscrupulous treatment of seamen, but it was not until 1890 that the Board of Trade were allowed to fix a loading line or Plimsoll mark stating how deep a ship could be loaded.

Improving navigation required not just an Act of Parliament, but a rise in the whole education standard. Many of the collier masters could not read or write which did not stop them from finding their way around the North Sea. Most people saw nothing unusual in this. After all, men had been navigating the sea long before a written language had been evolved. Also there was a feeling that some men were born to the sea. Humber pilot J. W. Duncan writing in 1905 expressed the opinion that 'keelmen are born, not made'. In other words everyone came into the world to take up a certain station and no amount of training altered this. It is true that basic personal characteristics are inherited, the rest are largely shaped by the environment and attitudes in which a person grows up. This means that a boy born into a maritime family and living in a maritime community would understand many of the ways of the sea, but this alone was not enough.

To be able to navigate properly a man had to master a complex skill involving mathematics. It was not terribly difficult but a navigator needed reasonably good navigational instruments and had to get his calculations correct if he was going to arrive at the right destination. Right up until the end of the sailing ship era navigation was not taken too seriously and the world was littered with wrecks which marked the spot where some master mariner discovered land unexpectedly. For a coastal master mariner to be seen spending too much time looking at a chart was taken as a sign that he did not know his job. Many writers have recorded instances of men who have sailed all their lives in the same waters and appear to develop a supernatural ability in the haven finding art. Press an old sailing coaster skipper for an explanation and he will look you straight in the eye and say that he could smell his way around.

Taking the rise out of curious people was almost as ancient a seafaring art as haven finding by experience. The sense of smell entered into this very little. The century old art of pilotage was based on knowing a particular area a good deal better than the back of your hand. The way the tide behaved, which landmark to look out for and the true compass course on every stage of the passage. This and much more was all learnt off by heart. It was actually an offence to destroy any buildings, usually windmills, towers and churches which were used by mariners as landmarks. After all, they stayed permanently still while the compass on an average coaster was not a very sensitive instrument. I have sailed with sailing barge skippers who have used only the traditional forms of pilotage and it does work surprisingly well. What did it matter if they took a little longer over a passage through wandering about the sea trying to pick up a landmark, or lose a few hours because they did not sail a straight course? They got there in the end. Indeed, considering the conditions under which the collier masters had to navigate, it is difficult to see how they could have done much else. There was no charthouse full of sophisticated navigation aids, just a tiny after cabin lit by an oil lamp and a few battered charts. What is more, in times of crisis they were so short handed that the master probably had to stay at the wheel (or in the case of the old collier brigs, at the huge tiller). Then all navigation had to be done in their heads. They were not superhuman; under such conditions they made mistakes, often serious ones.

For the coasting master navigation was the least of his worries. He was solely responsible for taking a wooden hulled sailing vessel, which made no progress beating against the strong wind, on a long passage with the help of a small and often indifferent crew. Not only was there the usual vile temper of the North Sea to be contended with, but the sea was then alive with small sailing ships. At night or in frequent periods of bad visibility these ships were poorly lit. Lamp oil cost money and masters often tried to please or cheat their owners by not lighting the lamps. The Board of Trade was for ever laying down the law about such things as navigation lights, but they were on shore. At sea they kept the lights burning low which saved a little oil, but caused an awful lot of collisions.

Britain's merchant shipping numerical supremacy has always been accredited to the Royal Navy's apparent control over the seas. Certainly that helped, but so too did the unlimited source of coal. Black diamonds they used to call coal, an indication of just how valuable it was. Originally the coal that was shipped out of the North East ports went for house fires, but in the period we are covering it was the cheap energy which brought about the industrial revolution. From the ship owners' point of view it meant that it was possible to get a coal cargo to virtually any part of the world. Coal was very bulky to stow and on long passages it often ignited, but it was always available. The need for coal to be delivered cheaply to the remotest corners of the globe kept many sailing ships active until World War I.

The North East ports were virtually built for the coal trade, but as well as supplying freights they also produced a high proportion of the ships. In the days of the wooden ship building quite large ships were built on any waterside piece of ground with deep water for launching, by any reasonably competent shipwright. The coming of economic iron shipbuilding in the 1870s meant that ship construction became more technical and involved more capital. The builders of the North East, particularly those on the River Wear grasped the new techniques and were soon turning out ships not just for local owners but for London and dozens of small ports round the British coast. Michael Bouquet shows in *South Eastern Sail* how a Shoreham firm was regularly having small iron barques built at Sunderland. These barques were trading to the Antipodes as were the ships of W. J. & R. Tindall of Scarborough. They had once built their own wooden ships. Hicks, another Scarborough shipowner, also had his new sailing ships from the Wear. Most of these ships were simply hard worked merchant sail whose exploits have been lost in the mist of time. A few

Unloading potatoes at Mill Dam Quay, South Shields, 1910

made a more permanent mark like the clipper *Mirage* built by John Pile at Hartlepool in 1854 which made some fast passages in the China Sea trade and the beautiful passenger clipper *Torrens* built at Deptford, Sunderland in 1875.

The last wooden ship built at Sunderland was the *Coppername* built by Pickersgills in 1880. The next few years saw great expansion in trade with the colonies. Steamers had already dominated trades to the East via the Suez Canal, but they were uneconomical for voyages to Australia and New Zealand because they had to keep popping into port for coal. For these routes which made use of the world's wind system, small sailing ships staged something of a come back in the early 1880s. This created a definite boom for Sunderland yards which reached a peak in 1883 when 128 new ships were launched. When the steam ships began to invade even the trade wind routes the owners' answer was to place orders for even larger steel four masted barques. On the North East coast this reached the limit with the huge 3,400 ton *Andorinha*, but by the 1890s the interest of the owners who placed orders in the North East yards had turned to steam. The Clyde builders went on turning out a few big sailers for another decade and Germany, which did not have an abundance of cheap coal, kept trying to develop deep water sailing ships right into the 1920s.

The Northumberland coast is one of rocky headlands and bays of golden sand.
It is a beautiful coast although blasted by the piercing winds of the relentless
North Sea. Our glimpse back into the past starts at the mouth of the River
Tweed and moves south. Above is the Carr Rock and the south bank just inside
the entrance of the Tweed. An enormous amount of trade went over this small
narrow quay. Ice was brought from Scandinavia and stored here in the speci-
ally constructed ice warehouses just back from the Carr Rock. The ice was used
to preserve the salmon in the smacks when they raced south to the Thames
under a huge press of canvas. Later on fish was sent by rail.

Above opposite is a group of Berwick herring drifters being towed in after a
night's fishing. These luggers went to sea in the evening and returned to harbour the next morning. Below opposite are two large Berwick drifters, the *Iona*
and the *Nellie Wilson* with Berwick paddle tug *Black Prince*. The Berwick drifters
were very close in design to the fifies from the Firth of Forth. This hull design
spread south as far as Bridlington, but at Berwick and further south they were
called simply keel boats to distinguish them from the coble family.

The drifters followed the herrings round the coast using the nearest port to the shoals. Opposite below is Sandstell beach at Spittal in about 1890. The shore is lined with luggers from The Forth and St Ives and Berwick keel boats. Above the herrings are being gutted for pickle curing at Boston's Bay View Yard in the building behind the drifters at Sandstell in about 1885. The man in the middle is an Irish buyer and on the right is Robert Boston (the second). Prior to 1914 the herring curing industry was big business on this coast. Above the older slightly easy going method is being used. The curing process which was used until 1947 started with the herrings being sprinkled with salt while being tipped into the gutting trough, or 'farlan'. Women worked in crews of three, two gutters and one packer. The gutters cut the throat of the fish and removed the gut and gills and selected the fish for size and quality just in an instant. They were then roused with more salt in a large tub and the packer lifted them into the barrel and packed them belly up across the barrel. The tiers were crossed and liberally sprinkled with salt all the way up the barrel. After eight days the herring was fully cured. During the eight days the blood from the fish dissolved most of the salt and became pickle. Enough coarse salt was left to keep the fish apart and allow the pickle to circulate.

Opposite above is Berwick Fish Market about 1906.

The Tweed is the most prolific salmon river in the country. Above salmon netting is in progress at Tweedmouth in about 1910. The men are holding the nets over the stern of a salmon coble. Another of these can be seen on page 14 under the bow of the central Cornish drifter. The river salmon cobles are rather like the Norwegian clinker prams and are used right up the River Tweed for catching salmon.

Above opposite is a Berwick sea coble in about 1904. The sea salmon cobles are about 22 ft long, clinker built but flat bottomed. Actually the Lee family who built them at Spittal always called them punts. The sea cobles worked in the river mouth and along the seashore; their flat bottom and soft upturned bows rode the waves more comfortably than the conventional boat. Because they were constantly scraped on the bottom in the shallows these cobles did not last more than about thirty years. Below opposite is a sea coble at Spittal in the 1920s. The salmon fisheries date back to at least the Middle Ages and are still going strong today. Once the whole of the Tweed was divided into fisheries, two cobles to a fishery, seven men to a coble, two of which worked the coble.

Above is Holy Island with Lindisfarne Castle on the other side of the Oose. This was taken in about 1902 when herrings were still being cured and packed into barrels on the foreshore. Already some of the old keel boats have been turned into sheds on the foreshore where they still remain. In 1887 there were thirty-seven boats owned at Holy Island and eighty-three fishermen were employed on them. Below is Seahouses in the early 1920s by which time most drifters had small engines. The dozens of schooners and ketches which came down from Scotland to the coal ports usually kept inside of the Farne Islands and in a North Easterly gale they used to come in here for shelter. However, getting round the islands in poor visibility was a problem and many were wrecked when trying to round the Longstone Light.

Seahouses Harbour. 9554

Above is the entire coble fleet hauled up on the beach at Craster probably in about 1900 before the harbour was built. Below is Craster harbour full of drifters in about 1905, when the south pier had not yet been completed. Craster was famous for its smoked herring not only caught from the local cobles but the herring were also brought north from Alnmouth.

The two photographs opposite were taken at Alnmouth. Here the River Aln flows into the sea creating a small shallow estuary twisting behind the village perched on a sandy promontory. The group of fishermen at the top include Mr Stewart in the centre back row and it was from his son, 82 year-old Jack Stewart, that I was able to hear about the old days. When this was taken, in about 1905, there were eight mule cobles line fishing from Alnmouth. There was no bait available locally so that the fishermen used to have an agreement with the crew of the collier brigs which sailed to Holland from Amble to bring some back. Later the bait came by rail from Morecambe Bay and Kings Lynn. Here, as else-where on the Northumbrian coast the decline of longshore line fishing was blamed on large trawlers steaming through their long lines.

Although Alnmouth dries out there was in the early nineteenth century regular trade in here with grain from the South which was stored in several granaries before being taken to Alnwick. Tradition says that at least two small brigs were built at the harbour mouth in front of Victoria Cottages. One was the *Duchess of Northumberland* and the other the *Coquet Lass* which was floated off the slip on a high tide when partially built, but was finally completed.

The bottom view is of the bluff bowed brigantine *Peace* discharging on the southern side of the harbour under the Church Hill. The box lighter under her bow used to take timber across to the saw mill. Sometimes part of a timber cargo had to be off loaded into the box lighter from a ship anchored off Aln-mouth before they could even get it in. Although there is no record to support it, tradition says that the brigs *Joanna*, *Gloriana* and *Diana* traded more or less regu-larly into Alnmouth. Locally called the 'wood ships' it seems that the last to come in was the *Joanna* in 1896. She was lying in the same spot as the *Peace* in the photograph opposite and was partly discharged with timber when she rolled over into the channel and damaged her hull. After this no one would insure a freight into Alnmouth.

Above are colliers waiting to load coal at Amble. In the distance, looking up the River Coquet, Warkworth Castle can be seen. Amble and Berwick were comparatively small coal ports.

The cobles of North England are some of the finest seaboats in the world. Their unique hull shape allows them to survive in the appalling conditions met with when running ashore on an open beach or in a short and treacherous sea which piles up in most harbour entrances. Above is the *Mary Elizabeth* and other Northumberland cobles ashore at Newbiggin in July 1931.

The main characteristics of the cobles were that the sides turned inwards creating a pressure which prevented the water from coming over the side. More important was the deep forefoot under the bow which gripped the water so that the stern swung round and the coble could be beached stern first. This was only done in bad weather so that the high bows could meet the roaring breakers. The trouble was that the cobles wanted to do everything backwards. When being rowed, two men pulled in the normal way, but a third crew sat at right angles in the stern and rowed sideways. This was to counter balance the grip forward. They had no centreboard, only a long rudder (*Mary Elizabeth*'s is lying on the stern). This meant they had an indifferent performance when going to windward; also having all the grip forward made them positively dangerous when running in a strong wind. If pressed too hard they broached round sideways on to the sea and were quickly rolled over and sank.

Above two colliers, a brig and a brigantine are loading at the North Blyth coal
staiths in March 1896. To the right a
Scandinavian schooner dwarfs the barquentine *Hilda* of Faversham in the
Import Docks, Blyth. In 1874, of the 200
sailing vessels owned in Blyth, almost all
were in the coal trade. During the summer
many made voyages with coal to the Baltic
and timber home. By 1904 there were only
two sailing vessels owned in Blyth.

Most winters saw at least one sailing ship wrecked at the mouth of the Tyne. Here a tops'l schooner has got herself ashore at Cullercoats, just north of the Tyne mouth. Cullercoats was formerly a coal exporting harbour and had a thriving coble fishing fleet. Some of these can be seen drawn up on the cliff top behind the harbour.

Most craft came to the North East coast of England to collect coal or to catch herring. Above the barquentine *Waterwitch* is being towed with difficulty into the Tyne. Coal from the Tyne to the south was for centuries the largest single coastal trade in the British Isles. Until steamers took over the trade it was undertaken by hundreds of 'Geordie' brigs. The Geordies hailed mainly from Tyneside and the Wear, but Hartlepool and Blyth colliers were often included in this term.

Below is a view of sailing traders at Newcastle.

THE LOW LIGHTS, NORTH SHIELDS 23.

Above opposite herring drifters are being rowed into the Tyne. Below opposite is the harbour of North Shields packed with herring boats from Kirkcaldy. Above is the same scene from the other side of North Shields low lights.

In the days when the North Sea coal trade was undertaken by sailing colliers the Tyne mouth bar at Shields was the first obstacle they had to overcome before making the hazardous passage to the Thames. Before dredging it was possible for the pilots to wade across the river at low water. Deeply laden colliers often had to scrape their way over before slamming away south with another freight of 'black diamonds' to keep the house fires of London burning. When the wind was south easterly the colliers came down the narrow Tyne between its steep banks and waited until the wind went round to be in their favour. Then up came their anchors and the whole fleet put to sea. The Tyne bar and the sea to the south was then covered in sails. Not just the bluff bowed Geordie brigs, but schooners, ketches, broken down deep sea barques and anything which could be kept afloat long enough to make the Thames.

29

The view at the top opposite is of the four masted steel barque *C. B. Pedersen* being towed into the Tyne in 1928 by the tug *Great Emperor*. Directly above is a view of her crew giving the barque's mizzen upper topsail a neat harbour stow while discharging Australian grain. By the time these photographs were taken sailers like the *C. B. Pedersen* were already long out of date and were being recorded because they were oddities from the past. This barque is fairly typical of the large sailing ships which really had their heyday between 1890 and 1910. The *C. B. Pedersen* was used in the interwar years by the Swedes as a training ship and was finally run down and sunk in 1938.

Below opposite is Tyne Dock at South Shields in 1896. The small clinker built lighters in the centre are Tyne keels. The function of the keel was simple: they loaded coal at the mine staiths at the head of the Tyne then drifted on the tide, with some help from small square sails and oars to the lower reaches where the coal was transferred to waiting ships. Each keel loaded 21 tons and the North country ships were referred to by the number of keels it took to load them. The keels in this view were sometimes called Tyne wherries to distinguish them from the early carvel built keels. Apparently only three keels were left in 1915.

Above is the brigantine *Devonia* and traders at Newcastle. Below is the Tyne at North Shields with a Tyne keel to the right.

Above a standing topgallant yard schooner is making sail after being towed out of the Tyne. Below a topsail schooner is ashore after failing to make the Tyne entrance.

It was Sunderland's claim that more ships were built here than in any other town in the world. There were other areas, notably the Clyde which built more ships, but these came from yards in several towns. To take one year, 1869, when sail was at its peak. There were 942 ships launched from British yards and of these 124 were launched at Sunderland. Glasgow was the nearest rival with 107 but the three main Clyde centres together produced 161. Building demands fluctuated, but it seems that in the height of sail supremacy the North East ports from the Tyne to the Humber were producing roughly about a third of all the British merchant sail.

Below is the 214 ton brig *Thomas & Elizabeth*, built at Sunderland in 1841. She is one of literally hundreds of similar brigs produced on the North East coast in the first half of the nineteenth century for the coal trade. Ships were steadily growing bigger and opposite can be seen the next generation of sailing ships being built but these were still wooden. Above opposite is Robert Thompson's shipyard on the River Wear with Scotts Pottery in the background in about 1860. Below opposite is Mowbray Quay by the Wear which was the site of Shorts yard between 1850 and 71.

Below is the four masted barque *Drumalis* built by W. M. Pickersgill & Sons at their Southwick yard, Sunderland in 1890 for P. Iredale & Porter of Liverpool. She represents the final development of sail on the North East coast. The *Drumalis* was 310ft long and had a tonnage of 2,529. Another Pickersgill barque, the *Andorinha* was 3,400 ton and was the largest sailing ship built on the coast. Pickersgill also built the last sailing ship on the Wear, this was the steel barque *Margarita* launched in July 1893. She was only 172ft long and 527 gross ton. The departure of sail would hardly have been noticed at the time for most yards simply switched to building steamers for the same owners. The *Margarita* was too small for ocean trading and was shortly sold to owners in Australia and under the name *Constance Craig* was lost with all hands in 1907 while in the intercolonial trade.

William Doxford & Sons Ltd of Sunderland built steamers, sailing ships or whatever else anyone cared to order. They built several iron barques and full rigged ships in the early 1880s and then went over to large steel barques, which although intended as carriers rather than clippers still managed to make fast passages. The sailing ships reached their peak and faded from the seas relatively quickly. In the 1850s the best of the clippers were still to be built but barely forty years later the whole era was over. The Doxford's management must have known that sail was a thing of the past when the four masted barque *Dominion* was launched in 1891. She was only eight years old when she left Honolulu for British Columbia and was never seen again. Doxford launched their last sailer the *Manchester* in 1892 and after this there were no more orders.

Above is the wreck of the *Harriet Wandle,* a brig built at Sunderland in 1862. Looking back, it often seems strange that the North Country ports stuck so religiously to the brigs because having square sails meant that their worst point of sailing was against the wind. Yet in the North Sea the prevailing winds are now south westerly which to the colliers would have meant a head wind from the coal ports to the Thames. However the weather records indicate that in the first half of the nineteenth century the prevailing winds were from the North East. This brought in much more severe winters, but it meant that a square rigged collier could spread her sails to a fair wind for the run south deeply laden with coal. Gradually the weather pattern changed until in the Edwardian era the prevailing winds were southerly and the summers longer and hotter. It may be coincidence but as the winds slowly altered the brigs dropped out of favour. Of course the high labour requirement helped push the square riggers out of the coastal trades, but the final sailing colliers were schooners, ketches and barges which could beat quite well against the wind.

In the view above two fishing luggers are being towed out of the Old Harbour entrance at Hartlepool. Opposite below is a collier brig being towed out and a herring lugger sailing in with a fair wind at the same spot.

The medieval walled town of Hartlepool sat on the headland overlooking the entrance of the River Tees. Behind the fishing boats can be seen part of the town wall surrounding the Old Hartlepool. This peaceful fishing village received a rude awakening when a railway company established the Victorian town of West Hartlepool on the opposite side of the bay and stole a march on the old town by opening an enclosed dock with a lockgate. The next forty years saw continual dock building and eventually the rival dock systems linked up. The port was born of the strange mixture of sharp business practices and idealism which somehow blended to make the highly successful Victorian England. By 1855 there were 192 sailing ships owned at Hartlepool and in the twenty-nine years between 1837 and 66 at least 114 were built here.

Above is the Hartlepool brigantine *Alexandra* owned by T. D. Pattison. Below is the Hartlepool ferry in about 1895. Two ferry routes, the old and the new, crossed Hartlepool harbour, saving about a mile walk between the Middleton shipyards and the engineering works and the old town on the headland. During World War I over a thousand men were ferried across each day and works lunch hours were staggered to allow men to get home and back.

Above is the mule *Matthew & Ellen*, owned by Will Allen, on the Fish Sands near the Old Pier, Hartlepool. Below are the cobles on the Fish Sands under the houses of Old Hartlepool.

Above sailing barges are loading sand at the Snook on the north bank just inside the Tees entrance. Below the Tees pilot Lithgo is returning home to Seaton Carew in his coble. Members of the Lithgo family have held Tees Pilots Licences continuously from about 1760. Pilot cobles were always painted black on the North East Coast. As well as working off the beach at Seaton they also congregated at Paddys Hole, a cove created during the dumping of slag from the local foundries to form the South Gare breakwater. Tees pilots also worked off the beach at Redcar and used to go down the coast as far as Whitby looking for ships. These cobles were rowed as much as they were sailed.

Above is a four masted barque in a Teeside Graving dock. The first four masted barque appeared in 1878, but the rig did not become popular until the 1890s and was the ultimate in the development of the large sailing ship.

At the beginning of the nineteenth century the River Tees was still surrounded by green rural countryside. A few ships made the hazardous passage up to Stockton which was then the main port. The Tyne already had a thriving coal trade and the Humber was an outlet to the industrial midlands. The Tees was transformed into an industrial area after the railways linked it to the coal fields in the 1830s. After this there was no looking back and wharves and ship-yards mushroomed up along the Tees. Stockton quickly proved too shallow and the new port of Middlesbrough sprang up on the Yorkshire side.

Above are a brig and brigantine discharging wheat in sacks into a keel at Stockton. Below is a barque frozen in the Tees during the great frost of 1860. Her timber cargo is having to be carried ashore across the ice.

Above a steamer is being launched from Craig Taylor's yard in about 1910.
The hull shape is very similar to the barque on page 43. Below is the Tees after
1885 with Craig Taylors in the centre back and R. Cragg's shipyard to the left.

Above is the brig *Griffin* ashore after being driven through Coatham Pier during a gale in 1873. The south shore of Tees Bay was a particularly bad place for wrecks because of the off lying shoals. These shoals meant that the Redcar fishermen had to combat surf long before they got anywhere near the beach. Because cobles were heavy to handle they were not popular here and Redcar men often favoured a lighter double ended boat. In the sailing coble days Redcar men were mainly lobstering and foying in the summer. This foying meant attending to weatherbound ships and taking holiday makers on trips. When engines were introduced, Redcar fishermen could work all the year round. Also the motor cobles tended to be larger than the old sailing cobles because they did not have to be rowed. There was never such a thing as a standard coble; they varied at each fishing centre to meet local conditions and to suit each individual fisherman's preference.

Both these views are of the barquentine *Ovenbeg* after she was driven ashore at Saltburn on 7 May 1924. By the 1920s commercial sail had virtually finished on the North East coast although a few traders from other regions of Britain and the Baltic still turned up from time to time. The Geordie collier brigs had held their own until the 1880s but by 1900 steamers had driven most of them out of the coal trade.

The main North Yorkshire fishing centres were Redcar, Staithes and Whitby. Around 1900 there appear to have been about fifty cobles owned in each of these. Above is Staithes and below a fisherman at Staithes is cleaning his day's catch ready for selling. Opposite the Ketch *Diamond* of Scarborough is discharging coal on the beach at Sandsend, just north of Whitby. Below are the Penzance men gathering at Whitby for the herring fishery.

Above is the collier brig *Opal* laid up at Whitby. Opposite is a view of a Penzance drifter and topsail schooner lying on the mud in Whitby.

After Redcar the Yorkshire coast is virtually a line of cliffs and the only port is Whitby where the tiny Esk estuary just manages to form a harbour at the bottom of a valley. In the eighteenth century Whitby was a port of considerable importance and between 1753 and 1837 whaling ships were owned here. By the late nineteenth century only a few colliers were owned here. The *Opal* above had been built at Greenock in 1845 and was owned at Whitby by G. Hopper who also had the 200 ton brig *Mary Stowe*. Another Whitby brig was the *Rachel Lotinga* which was built at Sunderland while the *Danube* was built and spent most of her career here.

The iron ore mine near Whitby lead to the construction of the tiny Port Mulgrave. This was built at the bottom of a 300 ft cliff and was connected to the mine by a mile long tunnel. Coasters came in to the harbour at high water to load ore, mostly for Middlesbrough.

Above Scarborough is seen crammed with shipping in the 1850s. The nearest topsail schooner is the *Little Henry*. The two views opposite were taken at Scarborough in about 1900. In the top view is the harbour lying below the shelter of the headland with its imposing castle. On the right is the stern of the billyboy ketch *Madam* of Goole and outside her is the trading smack *Grace*. The soft rounded bows and upward tilted bowsprit above the rail seems to have been a feature of the Scarborough traders. The hulks of two collier brigs are in the centre and the white lute stern of a Scarborough yawl can be seen near the ship-yard.

Below opposite is the hulk of a mid-nineteenth century brig. The interesting points are how small the cargo hatches are and how prominent the pumps and its wheel. The crew must have spent many hours working that pump.

The last sailing ship of any size built at Scarborough was the barque *Teviot* built by Tindalls in 1859. However small ocean wanderers like the barques *Arabella* and *Cumbria* were owned here until the 1890s.

The golden sands of Scarborough Bay attracted visitors early in the nineteenth century and this influx of the gentry created a ready demand for fresh fish. Local opinion however was against fish being landed here because the smell upset the visitors. Instead, Hull and Grimsby became the important fish landing ports of this coast. In spite of local resentment Scarborough had a sizeable fishing fleet. The early nineteenth century drifters here were three masted luggers, but these developed into ketch rigged vessels known locally as yawls. Below is a Scarborough yawl, with the normal curved lute stern, being towed from Grimsby. She was probably engaged in the February-July line fishing season because there is a coble on the deck. Yawls were also owned at Filey.

The deck view of the yawl on the left was taken at Scarborough. The iron bar which can be seen across the deck is the horse to which the loose footed mainsail was sheeted.

Above a small Scarborough mule is returning to her berth in the harbour. There are lobster pots amidships and presumably the day's catch was destined for the dining room tables of one of the select hotels. Below is a view from the quay of Scarborough cobles in 1900. The mule in the foreground is the *Dora Ann* which is decked forward and among those behind is the *Bonnie Lass*. Like most of the coble family these boats carried two masts and used the small spare one as a bowsprit.

Above is a Scarborough herring mule, locally called a 'plosher', and a smaller sharp sterned mule entering the harbour. These herring mules were over 40 ft long and were decked forward of the mast. This one is the *Margaret*, (1881–1916) she has a bowline to keep the leading edge of the sail taut. Both of these craft clearly show how strong the Norse traditions were even in the early twentieth century.

The traditional fishing craft of Scotland, the North East coast and East Anglia all had their origins in the norse craft and from this same ancestory individual types evolved so that every harbour and village had its own individual craft. The fishermen were fiercely local in their outlook to everything, including speaking in dialects which were virtually incomprehensible to anyone from outside their home area. For all this the fishermen were often fishing for the same fish in the same sea and watched each other like hawks. With the limited resources at their disposal it could take decades, even centuries for each cautious improvement to evolve, but once a new method was proved it would spread quite quickly. The Scarborough yawls were very similar to the Yarmouth and Lowestoft drifters and it took quite an informed eye to distinguish the herring mules from the visiting Cornish and Scottish luggers.

Above are a mixture of yawls, keel boats and a coble off Scarborough during the 1899 herring season. Below is the Fish Market on the West Pier at Scarborough in about 1903. The Cornish luggers are lying in the harbour entrance and fish are being landed on the beach from the cobles. This was done to save paying harbour dues. The collier brigantines from Hartlepool also unloaded on the beach in fine weather to save paying.

Above are the cobles drawn up at the North Landing, Flamborough. Below is the coble *Dawn*, owned by T. Cowling, also at Flamborough.

Above are the smaller Yorkshire cobles used for working off beaches. Below some larger harbour cobles are coming into Bridlington. Even in quite a stiff breeze they have not bothered to shift the lug sail round to the leeward side of the mast.

THE HARBOUR, BRIDLINGTON

Above is Bridlington harbour on an Edwardian summer's day with the cobles doing a roaring trade taking holiday makers for trips. There is little wind so that the crew are having to use the special poles to punt out of the harbour. Opposite below the Bridlington coble *Doris* is returning with a crowd of trippers in about 1908. For this work seats were put down the middle and they reckoned to get in about thirty-six people. Opposite above is another of the coble family near the Old Spring Pump, Bridlington. Special coble oars can be seen lying in her which had broad beam centres with a hole in them so that they pegged on to the throle pins on the coble's side. At the bottom of the steps water in buckets is being collected by the crew of a trader. Fresh water was taken on at most ports like this.

Pointed stern cobles were common at Whitby, Scarborough and Filey, but at Bridlington they preferred the flat stern. However there were a few double enders at Bridlington which for some obscure reason were called 'jinnies'. Fishermen loved inventing their own terms for gear and every port evolved virtually its own language. The men of Flamboro' spoke what was almost a language of their own. While the term coble, which is pronounced cobble in Yorkshire possibly comes from the old Celtic word ceubal meaning just a boat.

The Northcountry sailors stuck very obstinately to brigs as their favourite rig for coasters. Above is the Dover-owned brig *William Cundall* entering the Humber. She was actually built in Canada in 1863. More typical of the collier brigs is the *Cholmley*, built at Whitby in 1853 and seen below at Bridlington when she was owned by G. Brambles of Hull.

# The Humber

The Humber estuary cuts deeply into the side of England and numerous small rivers flow into it. So much silt comes down from inland that the Humber, on the ebb, is a boiling mass of brown water sweeping down to the sea. The tide is so strong that a vessel was often rolled right over by the weight of the water if it ran ashore. However, the Humber and its tributaries offered a natural system for water-borne transport. A barge was needed to carry cargoes on short estuary voyages from Hull and then far inland to the industrial towns and riverside wharves. To do this the Humber keel was evolved. Below a group of keels are ghosting down the Humber, probably to pick up a freight in the Hull docks.

Because most cargoes had to be delivered or collected far inland up some narrow shallow waterway the Humber shipowners needed a craft which could load the maximum cargo in the minimum hull size. This meant that all the Humber craft had almost flat bows and equally bulky sterns so that the maximum cargo was transported on the shortest possible hull length. The bluff bowed coastal traders of the Humber were called billyboys. Originally they were sloops similar to the one leaving Grimsby, opposite top. The larger ones were topsail schooners, but in the 1870s billyboys rigged as ketches were built at Goole, Howden Dyke and Burton upon Stather. Opposite below is one of these; she is actually on the River Yare taking a coal freight to Norwich.

Above is the sloop billyboy *Hydro* bound out of the Humber with fertiliser for the Wash. Andersons of Howden Dyke had the billyboys *Nitro, Sulpho* and *Phospho* too. The *Hydro*'s skipper lived aboard with his wife and family and kept the billyboy up like a yacht. So as not to damage the deck the skipper wore slippers whenever possible and dock workers who came aboard in hobnail boots were received very coarsely indeed.

The Humber traders on both these pages have the same general hull shape, but none of these vessels are identical. Above are the market boats *Toft Newton* and *Bee* at the Ferry Boat Dock, Hull. The market boats had gaff mainsails and were smaller than the square sailed keels. The market boats were used by carriers on regular services to transport mixed freights to Hull from every water-side town and village.

The keels masters used their knowledge of local tide conditions as a form of motive power as much as they used their simple square sails. This was fine for a trip inland, but the lower Humber proved a little too much like the open sea for this simple technique so that Lincolnshire owners started putting gaff mainsails and foresails on the keel hulls. These were known as Humber sloops and there is one illustrated opposite.

Every year the Humber sloops took a day off to race in the Barton Sloop Regatta. Opposite is Captain Dannatt's Burton Stather built sloop *Emma* racing and below Arthur Foster's sloop *Lily & Maud*. In their normal trade the sloops had a crew of two, but on race day to get the best out of their sloops extra crew were carried. The sloops would beat to windward well and always went about, while the keels often had to wear round before the wind at the end of each tack.

The Humber sloops were either market boats or bulk carriers taking building materials from the Lincolnshire ports across to Hull. Above is the sloop *John & Annie* discharging coal at Franks brickyard at South Ferriby. The sloops had their halyard winches mounted on either side of the hatch coamings. One of these can be seen on the right.

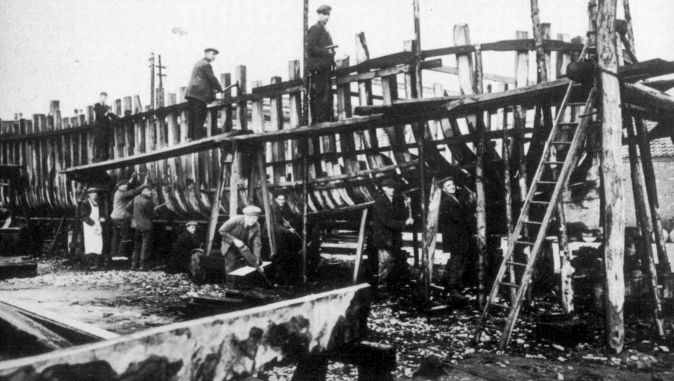

Above is the sloop *Alice* shortly before being launched from Brown & Clapson's yard at Barton-on-Humber on 24 June 1905. The smaller craft under construction just this side of her is a lighter. The *Alice* complete with all sailing gear cost £560 and was built to order for Joseph Oldridge of Barton. She was eventually lost when sailing out of the River Trent when she grounded on the Whitton Sand and sank.

Above opposite is the sloop *Mafeking* on her launching day, 4 May 1900 at Brown & Clapsons. Brown retired from this partnership in 1912 and the yard has since been run by four generations of Clapsons. Just how massively constructed the Humber craft were can be seen in the number of frames in the *Peggy B* being built here in 1935. She was ordered by Barton sloop owner James Barraclough and was the last wooden sloop built. In the Barton Regatta there were two classes, one for steel sloops and another for wooden ones. The course of this Humber sloop race was from Barton round the Grimsby Middle lightship and back, a distance of about sixty miles. The Regatta was keenly fought and aroused strong local feeling which drew crowds to Barton where the pubs stayed open long hours and a fair and stalls were set up. The race secretary confirms that the last Regatta took place in 1929.

The topsail schooner above leaving Bridlington has the pointed stern of a Humber billyboy. Below is the *Matilda* seen in a cold grey North Sea dawn. This topsail schooner was built by Banks at Selby in 1870 for Goole owners who kept her until 1900. The *Matilda* loaded 172 tons and had a crew of four men and a boy.

Below is the iron ketch *Mavis* built at Beverley in 1896, owned in Barton-on-Humber and sailed by Captain Aaron. She mostly traded between the Humber and the Wash and was later King's Lynn owned but stayed in the Yorkshire trade until 1938. In the 1950–60s she was trading around the Thames estuary as a motor barge and I remember seeing her in this rather unattractive role. The *Mavis* had very round bows and stern which marked her apart from the Thames sailing barges. Although most billyboys were slow and not very good sea boats, the *Mavis* had a good reputation as a sailer. For all this the *Mavis* did sink at least twice, once in 1927 after a Board of Trade survey at King's Lynn and again in her motor barge days when she rolled over in the Thames with a deck cargo of paper.

Billyboys were a compromise between a craft suitable for being towed through inland waterways and one which could make a sea passage. The *Mavis* in this view has her topmast housed and it would have had to be hoisted before the topsail could be set. Two of the four men on board are standing by one of the winches near the main mast, possibly waiting to hoist the topmast. Like most traders the boat is carried on the main hatch, well out of the way, but almost impossible to get over the side in an emergency. The last time I saw the *Mavis* she was lying abandoned against the seawall at Queenborough, Kent in 1971.

To keep fish fresh they were packed in ice which was imported from the Norwegian fiords. Left is a Norwegian ice barque being towed out of Grimsby. Below the man on the extreme left is hauling a block of ice with an iron scissor-type tool at the Grimsby Fish Dock.

Goole is some sixty miles inland from Spurn Head and was the largest of the inland ports on the Humber tributaries. It was normal for sea-going sailing vessels to be towed from Hull Roads up the River Ouse to Goole. Above the 647 gross ton barque *Teutonia* is being towed away from Goole in 1907 after discharging West Indian logwood. The tugs are the *Goole No 4* and *Goole No 5* while the Goole steamer *Mersey* is going up river behind them.

Goole was primarily a coal port, exporting mostly to European ports. It developed in the nineteenth century and by 1870, 457 ships were registered here, most of which were sailing vessels.

Above is the 237 gross ton barquentine *Golden Wedding* of Goole. A beautiful lofty trader which was the pride of Goole. Her white hull makes her look like a yacht, indeed she was in the world trade voyaging to romantic sounding places in the West Indies and South America. However, life aboard her was demanding. Captain Lee served an apprenticeship on her from 1901 to 5 and remembered that the food was confined to hard biscuit, salt beef, pea soup, rice and curry. The crew worked the cargo in and out so that there was little time off in port. On one passage she drifted helplessly for twenty-three days after losing her rudder. The *Golden Wedding*'s career, like most small sailers, was quite short. She was built by William Caisley at Howden Dyke in 1893 and was driven ashore and lost on the Mexican coast in 1907. This barquentine was ordered by George Kilner and, at the time she was lost, was owned by Caleb Kilner of Rotherham.

Below opposite is the Barge Dock, Goole in about 1890.

Above opposite is an attractive Baltic three masted topsail schooner, possibly the *G. R. Beig* at Gainsborough. Although she had been here before the schooner had such difficulties getting up the River Trent to this Lincolnshire port that the master refused to come again.

Above are keels at the Queens Staith, York and another below is being unloaded by wheelbarrow near Skeldergate Bridge c 1910. The keels were mainly bringing bricks to York and these were usually tossed ashore by hand. If the man on the bank missed the brick they fell into the water and at the end of the day the keel skipper stripped off and went in after the bricks. York is eighty miles from Spurn Head and the tide comes right up to Naburn lock, three miles south of the city.

Above is the keel *Robert Fox* at the Sutton-on-Derwent bridge at Elvington on the Yorkshire River Derwent. The shed in the background also belonged to Robert Fox. To reach a spot like this miles inland, the keel would have sailed if there was a fair wind. Otherwise she would have been hauled by her crew. Sometimes horses were hired from a farmer while on the busy waterways leading to the industrial centres there were regular steam packets for towing keels.

The keels spent most of their time away from the open water on the Humber estuary. Above opposite four keels are on the River Don at Doncaster. Below opposite are keels waiting at the entrance to Doncaster lock on the navigation at Doncaster. The keels penetrated the inland waterways right up to Sheffield and Leeds. Considering that the keels bow and stern was virtually flat to fit into the locks and that the only propulsion was a very simple square sail, they could sail remarkably well. Below are two passing each other in opposite directions on the River Trent. The light keel on the right has a man using a pole—the 'stower'—to help push her round the bend.

CROWLE WHARFE.

Above are keels at Crowle Wharf, North Lincolnshire in about 1908. At first glance these keels look rather clumsy vessels but I have found that the men who sailed them always speak highly of their ability. Notice on the keels above that the sail forefoot is hauled down taught on the weather bow so that the keels are sailing very close to the wind. The one in the foreground shows the bowline set up to the forestay to further help to keep the luff tight.

Opposite top is a sailing keel and the steam keel *Swift* at Thorne, Yorkshire in about 1908. Thorne was one of the numerous towns and villages in the West and East Riding which although many miles from the sea were deeply involved in maritime commerce. Thorne then got its drinking water from the waterways. The men on the keels also just dipped a bucket over the side for drinking water although wooden barrels were carried aft for fresh water while on the Humber. The keel opposite is far from salt water because she is on the Foss Dyke leading to Lincoln.

82

Canal, Thorne.

Above is a keel with her topsail set on the River Trent near Keadby in about 1910. Most keels had topsails, but they were only set in a light breeze. Opposite are two keels on the Foss Dyke Navigation which linked the River Trent to Lincoln. The first keel has timber stacked above the hatch coamings but the second keel had a heavier cargo and, because the Navigation was shallow, has had to off-load part of it into a lighter at Torksey and follow the normal practice of towing the lighter astern. Not only were the keels silent and picturesque, but they also left the waterways unpolluted.

Opposite are keels at Lincoln from Thorne and above, also at Lincoln, are keels drying sails.

The keels' chief centre of trade was Hull where they collected goods brought from all over the world. The return freight was usually coal to be loaded into outward bound ships. The keels also traded to Immingham and Grimsby. When bound inland the keel skippers thought of the waterways ahead as a left hand laid flat on the ground. The Humber was the arm, the thumb pointed up the River Hull through Hull's Old Harbour to Beverley and Driffield. The first finger was the River Ouse to Selby and York, the next to Goole, Wakefield and Leeds, the third finger was the River Don to Sheffield and the fourth finger led to Lincoln.

Above is a brig at the Fenland port of Wisbech on 25 June 1857. Below is Wisbech in the same period packed with locally owned and built ships, most of which were in the coal and Baltic timber trades.

Quite a few billyboys were owned in the Wash port of King's Lynn. Above is the billyboy *Evening Star*, built at Mexborough in 1873, at King's Lynn with several Dutch schooners. Below is the *Evening Star* after she had been run down by a steamer in fog in the Lynn Channel on 21 October 1905. The crew of three were drowned.

At the top of the tide a shrimper coming out of Boston, King's Lynn or the smaller Wash rivers would see a wide expanse of water. But long before low water that same craft would be hemmed in by high hills of sand. Since they were constantly beating up very narrow channels on comparatively smooth water, gaff cutter smacks were used. Above are some of the larger ones in Alexandra Dock, King's Lynn. Above opposite the Lynn fleet is coming out of Fisher Fleet and starting to beat down the River Ouse to the Wash. Below opposite are over thirty sailing smacks in Fisher Fleet in the 1930s.

Since few fish find their way into the Wash, local boats went after eels, shrimps and shellfish. The mid nineteenth-century Lynn boats had a clinker double ended hull, like the Norfolk beach boats, only larger and decked in except for a long open hatchway and had a gaff cutter sail plan. These were called yolls and were replaced by the shrimpers. The smacks on these pages are mostly shrimpers although a yoll can be seen in the background opposite below.

Fishing Fleet, King's Lynn

Above two Lynn shrimpers are attempting to make some progress rowing on the River Ouse. These have open hatches and flat counter sterns. The Wash smacks were built by Gostelows at Boston and Worfolk at Lynn. Nearly all had very fine bows and rather flat sides. The larger smacks had round counter sterns, this reached a climax when W. Worfolk launched the 58 ft smack *Britannia* on 8 April 1915 from his Friars yard, Lynn for Alfred Rake. She was the largest vessel launched at Lynn for forty years and the largest in the Lynn fisheries. In 1973 the *Britannia* was rigged as a yacht, but her contemporaries like the *Freda & Norah* are still working as motor craft.

You can travel the length of the coast between Berwick and King's Lynn, as I have done, and not see the mast of a single traditional working sailing vessel. The places are still there, some unaltered and some changed out of recognition but the everyday scenes in this book are as remote as the ice age. The above scene sums up the age of sail. Beautiful, backbreaking and slowly fading into the distance.

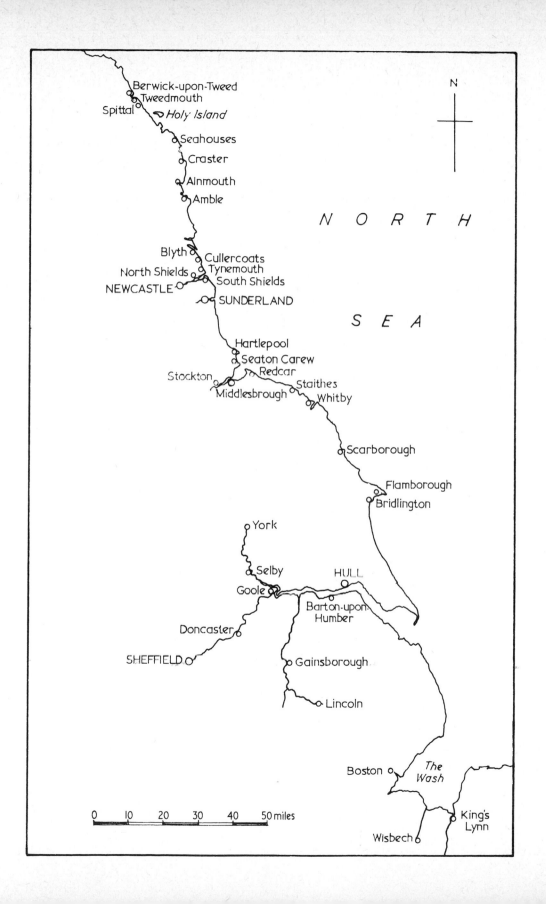

N

Berwick-upon-Tweed
Tweedmouth
Spittal
*Holy Island*

Seahouses

Craster

Alnmouth

Amble

NORTH

Blyth
Cullercoats
Tynemouth
North Shields
South Shields
NEWCASTLE
SUNDERLAND

SEA

Hartlepool
Seaton Carew
Redcar
Stockton
Staithes
Middlesbrough
Whitby

Scarborough

Flamborough
Bridlington

York

Selby
HULL
Goole
Barton-upon-
Humber
Doncaster

SHEFFIELD
Gainsborough

Lincoln

Boston
*The
Wash*

King's
Lynn
Wisbech

0    10    20    30    40    50 miles

# Acknowledgements

It has been my aim with this book to recapture some of the atmosphere of the age of sail without merely repeating that which has already appeared in other books. Most of the North East coast craft are referred to in works covering sailing ships generally; there is a photograph of the golddusters, a craft used by the Humber pilots, in *The Merchant Sailing Ship* by Basil Greenhill and Ann Giffard. So many people have helped to bring this book into being that it is hard to confine the thanks to a few people. Starting at the Tweed there was Mr Robert Boston of Spittal who introduced me to the local historian the Rev H. S. Ross. Sir John Craster gave details, not only of Craster but of fishing on the Northumbrian coast. Mr Jack Stewart of Alnmouth talked of events he remembered in his childhood in the 1890s. Mr R. M. Gard, the Northumberland County Archivist went to a great deal of trouble to find and help identify illustrations.

Further south Mr J. W. Smith allowed me to draw on his material for Sunderland and I am grateful to Mr D. M. Kimber, Chairman of Austin & Pickersgill, for his help. Far from the sea but also helpful was the Bowes Museum, Barnard Castle, and the curator Mr Michael H. Kirkby made the research easier here. On the Tees generally Mr R. G. Broderick of Hartlepool Maritime Museum willingly guided me in the right direction. From Scarborough, Captain G. V. Clark gave help. At Bridlington Mr S. T. Thompson from the Library aided this project while Mrs Maisie Lilley supplied information on cobles. Unfortunately there are few people around who used to sail cobles for a living, but on the Humber keels I am grateful to the keelmen who talked of the old days. Mr R. W. Cowl of York helped with photograph identification. Mr R. Clapson supplied details of his family's building yard at Barton and also from here Mr Ian Johnson and Mr R. F. Smith added their observations of the days of sail. On coasters Mr A. Bowes contributed with his memories at sea in the early 1900s. On the photographic side I am indebted to Mr Osbon of the National Maritime Museum and to Mr G. F. Cordy for making photograph copies.

On the world map the North East coast of England is just a dot, but if you set out to research and get to know this area you quickly discover that it is really a vast area. To find and identify photographs giving a reasonable coverage of this region required much travelling and time. I am fortunate in that my wife Pearl greatly helped with this, especially with the countless hours of typing and general background work needed to bring this book to life.

# Sources of Illustrations

The figures refer to the page numbers; the letters a or b indicate whether the picture is at the top or bottom of the page. Goole Public Library 1, 75, 76, 77b; Borough of Scarborough 7, 52, 53a, b, 56, 57a; National Martime Museum 37, 54a, 55a, b; South Shields Public Libraries 11, 27a, 30a, b, 31, 33a; Northumberland Records Office 12, 16, 25a, 32b; Robert Boston 13a, 14b, 15, 18b; Rev H. S. Ross 13b, 17b; A. H. Robinson 14a, 17a, 18a, 59a; Sir John Craster 19a, b; Mrs Baxter 20a, b; Newcastle upon Tyne City Libraries 22, 25b, 26a, b, 27b, 28a, b, 29, 32a, 33b; Graham Hussey 24, 57b, 63; Sunderland Museum 34, 35a, b, 36; R. F. Smith 8; Hartlepool Maritime Museum 38, 40a, 41a, b; Bowes Museum 39, 40b, 42a, b, 48a, b, 79; Langborough Museum Service 43, 46; Stockton-on-Tees Reference Library 44a, b, 45a, b; W. Belt 47a, b, 73, 89a, b; F. M. Sutcliffe 49a, 50, 51; Mrs F. Knights 49b; W. E. R. Hallgarth 54b, 59b, 64a, 67, 74a, b, 77a, 81, 82, 83a, b, 84, 85, 86, 87; Bridlington Library 58a, 60a, b, 61, 62b, 72a; C. E. Wilken 62a; Norwich Central Library 64b; Ian Johnson 65; Major Pickard 71; York City Library 78a, b; W. R. Roberts 58b; Doncaster Museum & Art Gallery 80a, b; Wisbech Museum 88a; Kodak Museum 88b; R. Clapson 66, 68a, b, 69, 70a, b; King's Lynn Library 90, 91a; Port of Lowestoft Research Society 91b, 92; Ian W. Milne 72b.